BLAZERS

Take Your (Equally Horible) Pick!

TAKE YOUR PICK OF

HAUNTED

PLACES

BY G.G. LAKE

CAPSTONE PRESS
a capstone imprint

Blazers Books are published by Capstone Press,
1710 Roe Crest Drive, North Mankato, Minnesota 56003
www.mycapstone.com

Library of Congress Cataloging-in-Publication Data
Names: Lake, G. G., author.
Title: Take your pick of haunted places / by G.G. Lake.
Description: North Mankato, Minnesota : Capstone Press, 2017. | Series: Blazers. Take your
    (equally horrible) pick! | Includes bibliographical references and index.
Identifiers: LCCN 2016035999 | ISBN 9781515744719 (library binding) |
    ISBN 9781515744757 (paperback) | ISBN 9781515744870 (ebook (pdf)
Subjects: LCSH: Haunted places—Juvenile literature. | Ghosts—Juvenile literature.
Classification: LCC BF1461 .L17 2017 | DDC 133.109—dc23
LC record available at https://lccn.loc.gov/2016035999

Editorial Credits
Nikki Potts, editor; Kyle Grenz, designer; Tracey Engel, media researcher;
Kathy McColley, production specialist

Photo Credits
Alamy: David Wall, 20, The Marsden Archive, 7; AP Photo: Dylan Lovan, 8; iStockphoto: Dieter
Spears, 5; Matthew Bordignon, 27; Shutterstock: Alexander Chaikin, 17, CREATISTA, 11, Everett
Historical, 15, Freedom Man, back cover and spine, Gordon Bell, 16, iolya, 24, Jacqueline Abromeit,
front cover (top), Jakub.it, 9, Karen Grigoryan, 13, MarcAndreLeTourneux, 12, Songquan Deng,
front cover (bottom); Superstock: Design Pics, 22; The Image Works: FrithMary Evans, 6; Wikimedia:
Cobra97/CC-BY-SA-3.0, 25, Constantin Barbu/CC BY 2.0, 18, Felix O/CC-BY-SA-2.0, 23, Nancy/
CC-BY-SA-4.0,3.0,2.5,2.0,1.0, 10, Pugin and Rowlandson, 1808/CC-PD-Mark, 21, Reading Tom/CC-BY-
2.0, 19, Shadowgate/CC BY 2.0, 14, Tim Kiser/CC-BY-SA-2.5, 26

Printed and bound in China.
007887

TABLE OF CONTENTS

Ghost Hunt..............................4

Athelhampton House or Borley Rectory....6

Waverly Hills Sanatorium
    or Alcatraz Island...................8

Woodchester Mansion or
    Winchester Mystery House 10

Edinburgh Castle or the White House 12

Culloden Moor or Gettysburg 14

Hampton Court Palace
    or The Tower of London.............16

Iulia Hasdeu Castle or LaLaurie House ...18

Empress Theatre or
    the Theatre Royal Drury Lane........20

Highway 666 or Pluckley Village 22

Highgate Cemetery or
    Bachelor's Grove Cemetery...........24

Trans-Allegheny Lunatic Asylum or
    Beechworth Lunatic Asylum..........26

Rapid Round 28

Glossary 30

Read More 31

Internet Sites......................31

Index.............................32

GHOST HUNT

Imagine you are a ghost hunter. You're ready for the hunt. In your pack are a flashlight, a cell phone, and a camera. If there's a ghost, you'll find it. There are so many places said to be **haunted** in the world. Take your pick!

haunted—having mysterious events happen often, possibly due to visits from ghosts

ATHELHAMPTON HOUSE OR BORLEY RECTORY

Would you pick Athelhampton House or Borley Rectory?

ATHELHAMPTON HOUSE

LOCATION: DORSET, ENGLAND

► Two ghosts fight with swords in the Great Hall.

► The Gray Lady haunts the east end of the building. A maid once saw this ghost walk through a wall.

► The ghost of a pet ape scratches the inside of the walls.

BORLEY RECTORY

LOCATION: ESSEX, ENGLAND

BACKGROUND: THE RECTORY BURNED DOWN IN 1939. TODAY GHOST HUNTERS STILL VISIT THE SITE.

▶ A nun's ghost walks the gardens looking for her lost love.

▶ In the 1930s a couple said a mean ghost attacked them. It broke windows and threw bottles.

▶ People **reported** seeing a ghostly **carriage** pulled by horses go through the gates.

report—a written or spoken account of something that has happened

carriage—a vehicle with wheels that is usually pulled by horses

WAVERLY HILLS SANATORIUM OR ALCATRAZ ISLAND

Would you pick Waverly Hills Sanatorium or Alcatraz Island?

WAVERLY HILLS SANATORIUM

LOCATION: LOUISVILLE, KENTUCKY

- ▶ A ghost named Timmy is said to live there. Timmy likes to roll balls back and forth with visitors.

- ▶ A ghostly old woman runs from the building. People have heard her scream "Help me!" and "Somebody save me!"

- ▶ During the 1900s workers got rid of dead bodies using a tunnel. Today voices and footsteps can be heard in the tunnel.

ALCATRAZ ISLAND

LOCATION: NEAR SAN FRANCISCO BAY
BACKGROUND: THE U.S. GOVERNMENT RAN A PRISON ON THE ISLAND FROM 1934 TO 1963.

- ► People have reported unexplained moaning, weird smells, and cold spots at the prison.

- ► Many workers have reported hearing banjo music play softly from the prison showers.

- ► According to American Indian **legends**, evil ghosts haunt the island.

legend—a story handed down from earlier times; legends are often based on fact, but they are not entirely true

WOODCHESTER MANSION
OR WINCHESTER MYSTERY HOUSE

Would you pick Woodchester Mansion or Winchester Mystery House?

WOODCHESTER MANSION

LOCATION: GLOUCESTER, ENGLAND

► A worker's dog is said to see the **mansion's** ghosts and lick their hands.

► A floating head scares visitors in the women's bathroom.

► The ghost of an old woman sometimes attacks young female visitors.

mansion—a very large house

WINCHESTER MYSTERY HOUSE

LOCATION: SAN JOSE, CALIFORNIA

▶ The 160-room house was designed oddly. Stairs lead to nowhere, and doors open to walls.

▶ Sarah Winchester, the past owner, haunts the room where she died.

▶ Visitors feel cold spots and hear voices of past servants.

EDINBURGH CASTLE
OR THE WHITE HOUSE

Would you pick Edinburgh Castle or the White House?

EDINBURGH CASTLE

LOCATION: EDINBURGH, SCOTLAND

▶ The ghost of a young boy bangs on a drum. It is said he only appears before an attack on the castle.

▶ Visitors to the castle say they have felt tugs on their clothing. They've also seen strange shadows.

▶ A friendly ghost dog haunts the castle's **cemetery**.

cemetery—a place where dead people are buried

THE WHITE HOUSE
LOCATION: WASHINGTON, D.C.

▶ The ghost of former president Abraham Lincoln haunts many rooms of the White House.

▶ The ghost of former president Andrew Jackson haunts the Rose Room.

▶ The ghost of past First Lady Abigail Adams has been seen hanging laundry in the East Room.

CULLODEN MOOR
OR GETTYSBURG

Would you pick Culloden Moor or Gettysburg?

CULLODEN MOOR

LOCATION: SCOTLAND, UNITED KINGDOM

BACKGROUND: A BLOODY BATTLE BETWEEN BRITISH AND SCOTTISH SOLDIERS TOOK PLACE HERE ON APRIL 16TH, 1746.

▶ Ghosts of dead soldiers haunt Culloden Moor. It is said the ghosts are most active on April 16th.

▶ Visitors can hear shouts and swords banging.

▶ A ghost of a Scottish soldier walks around saying "**defeated**" softly.

14 **defeat**—to beat someone in a war, fight, or competition

GETTYSBURG

LOCATION: PENNSYLVANIA

BACKGROUND: ONE OF THE BLOODIEST BATTLES IN THE U.S. CIVIL WAR (1861–1865) TOOK PLACE HERE.

► Present-day photos of Little Round Top hill show **orbs**.

► Ghost soldiers line up as if they are about to fight.

► In the Gettysburg College basement, ghostly doctors from the war help hurt ghost soldiers.

orb—a glowing ball of light that sometimes appears in photographs taken at reportedly haunted locations; many people believe orbs are signs of ghosts

HAMPTON COURT PALACE OR THE TOWER OF LONDON

Would you pick Hampton Court Palace or the Tower of London?

HAMPTON COURT PALACE

LOCATION: LONDON, ENGLAND, UNITED KINGDOM

▶ Past queen Catherine Howard haunts the palace **gallery**.

▶ The ghost of Sybil Penn, servant to four previous monarchs, haunts the state apartments and Clock Court.

▶ In 2003 what looked like a skeleton wearing a **cloak** appeared by a set of doors. It quickly disappeared.

gallery—a place where art is shown

cloak—a loose piece of clothing that is used like a coat or cape

THE TOWER OF LONDON

LOCATION: LONDON, ENGLAND, UNITED KINGDOM

BACKGROUND: ENGLAND HAS USED THE TOWER AS A PALACE AND A PRISON.

▶ Prince Edward V and his brother Richard were killed in the Tower. Today their ghosts appear wearing white and holding hands.

▶ Anne Boleyn's ghost has been seen running through the courtyard. The past queen was killed at the Tower.

▶ Visitors have reported feeling their throats being crushed.

IULIA HASDEU CASTLE OR LALAURIE HOUSE

Would you pick Iulia Hasdeu Castle or LaLaurie House?

IULIA HASDEU CASTLE

LOCATION: CAMPINA, ROMANIA

BACKGROUND: BOGDAN PETRICEICU HASDEU BUILT THE CASTLE FOR THE GHOST OF HIS DAUGHTER, IULIA.

▶ Hasdeu said he talked with Iulia's ghost in one of the rooms.

▶ Strange symbols appear on the walls. It's said the symbols help the living connect with the dead.

▶ Visitors have seen Iulia's ghost playing the piano.

LALAURIE HOUSE

LOCATION: NEW ORLEANS, LOUISIANA
BACKGROUND: MADAME LALAURIE TORTURED ENSLAVED AFRICAN-AMERICANS IN THE HOUSE.

▶ Ghostly footsteps can be heard in the house.

▶ Moans come from the attic where Madame LaLaurie hurt African-Americans.

▶ A young girl haunts the house. She tugs on visitors' clothing.

torture—to cause someone extreme pain or mental suffering

EMPRESS THEATRE OR THE THEATRE ROYAL DRURY LANE

Would you pick the Empress Theatre or the Theatre Royal Drury Lane?

EMPRESS THEATRE

LOCATION: FORT MACLEOD, ALBERTA, CANADA

- ► A janitor named Ed haunts the Empress Theatre. He sometimes sits and watches plays.

- ► A man's face appears in bathroom mirrors.

- ► An actor once reported that a ghost trapped him in the basement.

THE THEATRE ROYAL DRURY LANE

LOCATION: LONDON, ENGLAND, UNITED KINGDOM

▶ Many people have reported seeing a floating white head.

▶ Some people have reported being kicked in the rear by a ghostly clown.

▶ The ghost of a young man wearing a white wig and a gray cloak appears. He is called the Man in Gray.

HIGHWAY 666 OR PLUCKLEY VILLAGE

Would you pick Highway 666 or Pluckley Village?

HIGHWAY 666

LOCATION: SOUTHWEST UNITED STATES

- ▶ The ghost of a young girl appears on the side of the highway. She disappears when drivers try to help her.

- ▶ Evil ghosts are said to try to cause car crashes.

- ▶ A ghost truck haunts the highway. It's on fire as it speeds down the road.

NORTH

666

NORTH

666

► People say there are at least 12 ghosts in the town of Kent.

► The ghost of an old woman sits at a bridge. She has been seen smoking a pipe.

► A young, beautiful ghost haunts St. Nicholas's Church. She is called the White Lady.

HIGHGATE CEMETERY
OR BACHELOR'S GROVE CEMETERY

Would you pick Highgate or Bachelor's Grove Cemetery?

HIGHGATE CEMETERY

LOCATION: LONDON, ENGLAND, UNITED KINGDOM

▶ Lack of care after World War II (1939-1945) has left the eerie cemetery in disrepair.

▶ A ghost of an old woman screams for her lost children. She runs between **tombstones** looking for them.

▶ A man reported seeing a creature with glowing red eyes.

tombstone—a carved block of stone that marks the place where someone is buried

24

BACHELOR'S GROVE CEMETERY

LOCATION: NEAR CHICAGO, ILLINOIS

- ▶ A ghost carrying her baby haunts the cemetery. She appears during full moons.

- ▶ Visitors sometimes see a ghostly house.

- ▶ A ghostly farmer, horse, and plow haunt a nearby pond.

TRANS-ALLEGHENY LUNATIC ASYLUM OR BEECHWORTH LUNATIC ASYLUM

Would you pick Trans-Allegheny Lunatic Asylum or Beechworth Lunatic Asylum?

TRANS-ALLEGHENY LUNATIC ASYLUM

LOCATION: WESTON, WEST VIRGINIA

► A ghost named Ruth haunts the first floor. She pushes people who say her name.

► People have seen doors closing on their own in the **asylum**.

► The fourth floor is said to be the most haunted. People have heard unexplained voices and banging sounds there.

asylum—hospital for people who are mentally ill

BEECHWORTH LUNATIC ASYLUM
LOCATION: BEECHWORTH, VICTORIA, AUSTRALIA

► Visitors have heard ghostly screams and laughter.

► Matron Sharp is the asylum's friendly ghost. She wears a gray hood.

► An old ghost in a green jacket haunts the gardens.

27

RAPID ROUND

Which would you pick to play hide and seek in?

THE TOWER OF LONDON OR HIGHGATE CEMETERY?

Which would you go to for vacation?

WINCHESTER MYSTERY HOUSE OR PLUCKLEY VILLAGE?

Which would you live in with your family?

ATHELHAMPTON HOUSE OR LALAURIE HOUSE?

Where would you film a scary movie?

HIGHWAY 666 OR IULIA HASDEU CASTLE?

Which would you pick to clean?

THE WHITE HOUSE OR THE WINCHESTER HOUSE?

Which ghost would you like to meet?

THE **WHITE LADY** IN **PLUCKLEY** OR THE **MAN IN GRAY IN DRURY LANE** ?

Which ghost pet would you pick?

A **DOG** OR AN **APE** ?

Which would you pick for a picnic?

GETTYSBURG OR **BACHELOR'S GROVE CEMETERY** ?

Which would you pick for a sleepover with friends?

TRANS-ALLEGHENY LUNATIC ASYLUM OR **EMPRESS THEATRE** ?

Which would you rather hear?

GHOSTLY LAUGHTER OR **GHOSTLY FOOTSTEPS** ?

29

GLOSSARY

asylum (uh-SY-luhm)—hospital for people who are mentally ill

carriage (KAYR-ij)—a vehicle with wheels that is usually pulled by horses

cemetery (SEM-uh-ter-ee)—a place where dead people are buried

cloak (KLOHK)—a loose piece of clothing that is used like a coat or cape

defeat (di-FEET)—to beat someone in a war, fight, or competition

gallery (GAL-ur-ee)—a place where art is shown

legend (LEJ-uhnd)—a story handed down from earlier times; legends are often based on fact, but they are not entirely true

mansion (MAN-shuhn)—a very large house

orb (AWRB)—a glowing ball of light that sometimes appears in photographs taken at reportedly haunted locations; many people believe orbs are signs of ghosts

report (ri-PORT)—a written or spoken account of something that has happened

tombstone (TOOM-stone)—a carved block of stone that marks the place where someone is buried

torture (TOR-chur)—to cause someone extreme pain or mental suffering

READ MORE

Polydoros, Lori. *Top 10 Haunted Places*. Top 10 Unexplained. North Mankato, Minn.: Capstone Press, 2012.

Raij, Emily. *The Most Haunted Places in the World*. Spooked! North Mankato, Minn.: Capstone Press, 2016.

Tieck, Sarah. *Ghosts*. Creepy Creatures. Minneapolis: Abdo Publishing Company, 2016.

INTERNET SITES

FactHound offers a safe, fun way to find Internet sites related to this book. All of the sites on FactHound have been researched by our staff.

Here's all you do:

Visit *www.facthound.com*

Type in this code: 9781515744719

Check out projects, games and lots more at
www.capstonekids.com

INDEX

Adams, Abigail, 13
African-Americans, 19
American Indians, 9
apes, 6
asylums, 26–27

battles, 14–15
Boleyn, Anne, 17

car crashes, 22
castles, 12, 18
cemeteries, 12, 24–25
Clock Court, 16
cold spots, 9, 11

dead bodies, 8
dogs, 10, 12

East Room, 13

Gettysburg College, 15
ghost hunters, 4, 7
ghost trucks, 22

Gray Lady, 6

horses, 7, 25
Howard, Catherine, 16

Jackson, Andrew, 13

Lincoln, Abraham, 13

Man in Gray, 21
Matron Sharp, 27

nuns, 7

Penn, Sybil, 16
Prince Edward V, 17
prisons, 9, 17

queens, 16, 17

Rose Room, 13

soldiers, 14, 15
St. Nicholas's Church, 23
symbols, 18

theatres, 20–21
tunnels, 8

U.S. Civil War, 15
U.S. government, 9

White Lady, 23
World War II, 24